Winning
Ways

G. P. Putnam's Sons
New York

Winning Ways

Four Secrets for
Getting Great Results
by Working Well with People

DICK LYLES

WITH A FOREWORD BY
KEN BLANCHARD, PH.D.

G. P. Putnam's Sons
Publishers Since 1838
a member of
Penguin Putnam Inc.
375 Hudson Street
New York, NY 10014

Library of Congress Cataloging-in-Publication Data

Lyles, Richard I.
Winning ways / Dick Lyles.
p.   cm.
ISBN 0-399-14606-7
1. Psychology, Industrial.   2. Interpersonal relations.   I. Title.
HF5548.8.L95   2000   99-058057
650.1'3—dc21

Printed in the United States of America
1   3   5   7   9   10   8   6   4   2
This book is printed on acid-free paper. ∞

Book design by Deborah Kerner

To Mom and Dad, whose unconditional love has inspired me throughout my life. No one is better at building winning relationships than Mom.

To my soul mate, lover, wife, partner, and best friend, Martha. You are my greatest blessing. You are my soul and inspiration. I love you more than all the trees.

To Jennifer, Whitney, and Chip, for the love you show to Mom and me, each other, and the world. No one could be more proud of their offspring than I am of you. Thanks for your support—words can't describe how much it means to me.

ACKNOWLEDGMENTS

First and foremost I extend my heartfelt thanks and deepest appreciation to Ken Blanchard, Sheldon Bowles, and Spencer Johnson, for their guidance, coaching, teaching, and support. These "masters of the modern-day parable" have been gracious and giving, sharing both their time and their immense wisdom willingly, openly, and without reservation. I pray that at least some portion of what I learned from them is reflected on these pages.

Thanks to Margaret McBride, my literary agent, and her team for their efforts in helping to transfer this dream into reality.

Thank you, Putnam, for affording me the privilege of

working with Denise Silvestro, clearly one of the finest editors in the business.

And special thanks to the many others who have helped each in their own way to make this book come alive. They include Leslie Gelbman, Mary Ann and Carl Weegar, Eunice Parisi-Carew, Scott Blanchard, Art Bauer, Mario Tamayo, Hugh Goldie, Cathy Conheim, Drea Zigarmi, Marsha Wilson, Martha Bushko, Susan Fowler Woodring, Harry Paul, Todd MacDonald, Dick Vortmann, Eileen Haag, Marilyn Ducksworth, Dan Harvey, Barbara O'Shea, and Ron Olson.

And most important, thanks to my family for your love and support, without which this book would not have been written.

Unleash More of
Your Power Today

A FOREWORD BY

KEN BLANCHARD, PH.D.

CO-AUTHOR OF

The One Minute Manager®

In thousands of conversations I've had with people all over the world since writing *The One Minute Manager*®, one universal concern has been driven home repeatedly. People worry about the huge amount of creativity that is wasted—lost forever—because talented people are prevented from giving their best by their lack of ability to influence others effectively.

Today's workplace is teeming with people who have terrific ideas, a great deal to contribute, and for whom computers and technology are as natural as the air they breathe. However, a large number of these people are not operating at peak performance because they are unable to work well with others and successfully present and implement their ideas.

At one time or another we've all experienced the frustration that arises when we are unable to influence others in a positive and effective manner. In *Winning Ways,* Dick Lyles gives us four very powerful strategies that all of us can use to improve our relationships with others and increase our own level of success. These are the best guidelines I've seen to help you unleash your power and reach your maximum potential.

The business world has changed; organizations are getting flatter and more networked. Today, the key to success is one's ability to exercise peer leadership. The most successful individuals shine because of their ability to influence, empower, and energize others. In essence, they embody the principles and practices of *Winning Ways.*

As you study these ideas, think about two dimensions we must always be concerned about when we think of leadership at any level—chemistry and successful execution. Leadership won't work unless the chemistry between leaders and followers is healthy, vibrant, and positive. Nor will it work if mutually satisfying results are not achieved. The principles of *Winning Ways* are especially exciting because they provide a solid foundation for both, with a focus on peer leadership.

This is the kind of book you will pass along to others and you'll want to read it over and over again. And if you're like me, you'll remember these ideas and apply them your-self in your daily interactions. The sooner you do so, the sooner you'll find yourself on a permanent path toward developing truly *Winning Ways* in all your dealings with others.

KEN BLANCHARD

Winning
Ways

Albert was livid. Absolutely livid.

"How could they?" he said to himself. "How could they ask me, how could they ask anyone with any intelligence whatsoever, to put up with this kind of treatment?"

The young man was seething as he slammed into his chair and assaulted his computer. If the mouse had been a live one, it surely would have suffered whiplash from Albert's jerking as he whipped it back and forth across the mouse pad to disengage his computer's screen saver and cause the menu display to pop onto the screen.

Albert quickly scrolled the cursor to his Internet browser icon and double clicked. He tapped his right heel up and down and glared off into the opposite side of his office cubicle, fuming as he waited for the computer to bring up his designated home page.

His anger slowly gave way to fear and a deep, gut-wrenching anxiety as he continued to reflect on what had just happened. His stomach began to tie up in knots as he realized that his second experience in working with groups had quickly become worse than his first.

The first "Tiger Team" they had assigned him to had been bad enough. But fortunately—both for Albert and the other team members—the assignment had been a short one. The work was for the most part completed by the time Albert joined the group. Albert's contribution wasn't critical to the outcome, but was important to the project's overall success. The good news was that although Albert's piece was indeed challenging, it didn't require too much collaboration with the others on the team.

From the beginning Albert felt that the other Tiger Team members weren't very friendly. They were congenial to each other, but never really warmed up to him. Even more important, though, he felt they didn't show enough respect for his intellect or his ideas. Deep down inside he knew he was smarter than all but one, and he could certainly hold his own with her. Worse yet, they were almost arrogant about the work they had already accomplished, even though Albert was confident he could have done a better job.

However, strained feelings and underlying tensions

aside, the team and Albert finished the project before anyone's emotions festered to the boiling point. Albert went
back to his own work, relieved the project was over. He was
thankful he could work alone without having to worry
about all the hassles, frustrations, and endless, time-
consuming delays of dealing with a bunch of groupies who
were more interested in what everybody else was doing than
they were in getting the job done.

Then came this second Tiger Team.

Even the term Tiger Team rubbed him the wrong way.
What was it supposed to mean? Albert suspected it was just
a form of manipulation to get people to think they were
special if they did something with a bunch of other people.

Well, Albert didn't feel special. In fact, working in a
group just gave him a headache.

*Why couldn't they just tell people what was needed, divvy up
the work, and then let them go do it?*

No, that'd be too easy, he reflected.

Albert's frustration with this second team had set in
early. The team had started off in what Albert considered to
be the wrong direction. He thought they were trying to satisfy too many people with the design, thereby making the
finished product much too complicated.

When they told him they had to follow that approach
because it was specifically spelled out in the team's charter,
he clammed up. *Have it your way,* he thought smugly to himself. *You'll see.*

The next uncomfortable moment was triggered in the team's second meeting when Albert told the team leader his name was "Albert—not Al. Two syllables, not one." He momentarily felt a little guilty that the team leader had been embarrassed when Albert corrected him in front of everyone. But only a little guilty. He thought it insulting that the guy couldn't even refer to him by his correct name.

And now this.

Each of the team members had agreed to complete an assignment during the three-week time period between the second and third meeting. Then they would get back together at the third meeting and piece things together to lay the foundation for the rest of the project.

After starting his work according to the criteria that the group had agreed upon, Albert came up with a better idea. He refocused his efforts and put all his energy into developing this new idea. For the past two weeks, he worked day and night, and even gave up both weekends. With the exception of a couple of hours on Saturday and Sunday when he played Frisbee with his pet Australian shepherd, Digger, he worked nonstop. He was eager for everyone to see how much better his plan was.

He prepared a presentation to deliver to the group at the beginning of the third meeting. He even titled it "A Better Way," so they would get the point quickly and not waste any more time following the mediocre direction they had originally—and by Albert's judgment, mistakenly—

taken. He even rehearsed the presentation a few times in front of Digger, who enthusiastically barked his approval.

Albert had stayed up all night working to fine-tune his speech and was in the office early that morning, eager to present his ideas to the other team members.

Then came the meeting.

As soon as the group had exchanged their usual pleasantries, Richard, the project leader, outlined his agenda. Albert interrupted to ask if he could take a few moments to address the group before they started work on the agenda. He assured them they'd be pleasantly surprised and would consider it time well spent.

The group consented.

Albert proceeded to outline his ideas and the plan he had spent the past two weeks perfecting.

To say the presentation didn't go well would be a considerable understatement.

As soon as he started to explain how his idea was superior to the one the group conceived, the team members began to withdraw. Some folded their arms. Faces turned serious; some were even grim. The overall reaction was decidedly negative.

When team members started questioning the reasons for some of Albert's suggestions, Albert became defensive and pushed even harder to convince the group that his way was a better way. He raised his voice, impatient to get his point across, but the louder he spoke, the louder the dissenting team members protested. The meeting quickly became a classic power struggle.

And Albert lost. Big time.

He not only lost the argument, but he lost his cool.

Albert's composure was annihilated as he stormed out of the conference room in a huff—an angry, contemptuous huff—that left a wake of ruffled emotions and unresolved conflict.

So now here he was. Mindlessly surfing through cyberspace, contemplating his situation, and wondering why some people were so hard to get along with.

Albert longed for a return to the days when he was in college. Albert had graduated *cum laude* from the University of Northeastern Michigan (UNM) with a bachelor of science degree in computer engineering. He graduated in three years instead of the usual four or five like most students these days. Albert would have been the valedictorian the year he graduated had it not been for his less-than-stellar grades in his humanities classes. In the classes he really liked—those that focused on computers, math, and science—the college classroom environment served him well. He studied hard, went to class, locked into each professor's delivery, and filed away everything he learned in his computer-like brain. Albert could memorize formulas, equations, and programs, and could always come up with the right answers. He would do his work, study hard, and was solely responsible for his academic success.

At graduation time Albert was recruited heavily and was quickly hired by United Global Advance Technologies, better known as UGAT. UGAT is a Chicago-based high technology company with worldwide operations. He settled in quickly and rapidly gained notoriety as the company's brightest rising star.

Ten months later he was assigned to his first Tiger Team. The team was brought on board to help complete the company's hottest and most important project.

Albert felt his contribution was minor because he was put on the project so late in the game, but because he crossed the finish line with the group, he was included in the recognition for the project's success. In fact, he even received special recognition for getting up to speed so quickly and helping out at the last minute.

That's why Albert's department head, Megan Godwine, had assigned Albert to be on this current project from the beginning. It was a terrific opportunity—one that would have normally been reserved for a more senior and experienced person. But Albert had established himself with his work on the first team and Megan felt this second team would be a great chance for him to proceed on the fast track. Megan seemed to genuinely want to see Albert succeed. She was the person who recruited him and urged him to come on board at UGAT. She was also a graduate of

UNM and in fact had first learned about Albert through her old professors. As a department head, she was constantly on the lookout for top talent, and the professors knew it. They enthusiastically recommended Albert to her and Megan immediately recognized his potential. Now she offered him what she thought to be the opportunity of a lifetime and he wanted out.

What should I say when I meet with her in the morning? Albert asked himself. He and Megan had an appointment scheduled for 8:00 A.M. so he could debrief her on the project and how it was going.

Until now he had been looking forward to the meeting, confident he'd be able to tell her all about how he had reshaped the project direction and really made a difference. But now all he could think about was how to tell her he wanted a different assignment.

He couldn't work with these people. Not now. Not after they had completely humiliated him by rejecting his ideas without even so much as a hint of reasonable consideration. *Why couldn't they just put their egos aside and listen, even just a little? Most of them had stopped listening in the first three minutes! There's no way she could expect him to take that. It was a sign of disrespect and an indication that they didn't want to work with him.*

Maybe it's because I'm still one of the new people around here, he thought. *But it's wrong for them to treat me that way, even if I am new. Besides, don't they get it? It's the ideas that matter, not me. I'll bet if any one of them had the same idea, they'd think it was great. They're just intimidated by someone my age being so far ahead of them. They're trying to teach me a lesson, make me pay my dues.*

Well, they can have their lesson, he thought. *Tomorrow when I meet with Megan, maybe I should just tell her to tell them that they can take that attitude and my job on this Tiger Team and shove it.*

One thing he was certain of was that he was not going to let Megan think any of this was his fault. Even though he suspected that the knot in his stomach was at least partly caused by the knowledge that in some way he had provoked the team's reactions, he didn't want to admit that to Megan.

No, he thought. *In as polite and respectful a manner as possible, I'll just ask her to take me off the team. Maybe there's another team with different people she can assign me to. But what I'd really like to do is work alone.*

Albert went home and took Digger for a romp in the park. However, playing with Digger didn't take his mind off his problems. After a sleepless and fitful night, Albert showed up at Megan's office at 8:00 sharp, dreading their meeting but wanting to get it over with.

Albert had developed two possible lines of reasoning to present to Megan about why it would be better for him to not continue with the Tiger Team.

First was that he didn't fit in because of his age. The other team members were all older, had been with the company longer, and considered themselves more experienced. Second, his intelligence made others jealous and competitive. It was obvious that he was smarter than most of them. His superior intelligence made it hard for them to accept him. He had run into this before. As soon as he opened his mouth, others would try to one-up him to prove how smart they were. People felt threatened by him, which often resulted in a battle of wills and feelings of resentment. This was exactly what was happening with this Tiger Team.

The problem was he didn't think it would be good to share either of these thoughts with Megan. Definitely not the intelligence theory. He knew from experience that if he raised *that* issue the conversation would most likely shift from intelligence to ego and all that psychological stuff that he hated. *Besides,* he thought, *I don't have any ego problems. All I want is to be able to do a good job and have everyone else do a good job, too.*

He didn't want to get into the age issue, either. He'd always been ahead of his age. He was typically the youngest person in most of his technical classes. Over time he'd come to expect that a few people in every group would resent him being so bright and young. Long ago he had decided to ignore them. If they had a problem, let it be their problem. He wasn't going to let it be his.

Why is it so hard to connect with other people? he asked, for at least the thousandth time in his life. *Why don't other people get frustrated trying to get their ideas across? Or do they?* Again, as he had many times before in his life, he retreated quickly from this line of thought. No sense wasting time in speculation.

After saying good morning, he started by telling Megan that after having been to a few of the Tiger Team meetings, and looking at the work the team was pursuing, he felt his talents could be better used elsewhere. He even had a proposal for a new project he could work on by himself. It took him about ten minutes to explain all this, while Megan just listened. She was a good listener, asking questions to clarify certain things Albert had said, and she took a lot of notes.

When Albert was finished outlining his proposal, he asked what she thought.

"Well," she responded, "I'm somewhat surprised at what you're proposing. But I was warned that you wouldn't be feeling totally pleased about the way things are going."

"What do you mean?" Albert responded. "I've been working hard on this project."

"I know. I've noticed. But Richard called me at home last night to tell me about yesterday."

"It's no big deal."

"Richard has some major concerns. He said the whole team was upset, and that you got really emotional."

"That's all the more reason my proposal makes sense.

Richard can find someone else to do my job, I'll go work on this other project, and everyone will be happy."

"It's not that easy, Albert. Richard said that as the project manager, he's had concerns about your ability to get along with the team members since the beginning. He was going to wait for one more meeting to come and talk to me, then this happened. But this is not something we can call just not getting along. What happened yesterday is much more serious."

"So what does that mean? Are you going to fire me?" Albert's impatience began to show.

"Whoa, not so fast." Megan was caught off guard by Albert's cutting reply. "We need to talk about this."

"There really isn't that much to talk about." Albert answered back. "Your Tiger Team wants to do its thing without me, and I like working by myself, so why not just do it that way and make everybody happy?"

"Because I wouldn't be happy, and the company's needs wouldn't be getting met."

"I don't get it."

"Albert, you were assigned to the team for two reasons. First, because of what you can contribute to the project, but second, because it's a nice career step for you."

"I'm not the only one who can contribute. And besides, they don't want my contribution. So why not get somebody else? Isn't that the easiest way?"

"The easiest way isn't always the winning way," Megan

explained. "It's my job to see we do things the best way possible."

"Best for who?"

"If it isn't good for everyone, and especially the company, then it probably isn't the right way for anyone."

"What about me? Do I count as part of everyone? Because if I do, I'd just as soon work by myself."

"You're definitely part of everyone. But it sounds to me like you really need to think through your perspective—by that I mean how you relate to everyone and what the nature of your relationship should be."

"What's wrong with 'I do my work and they do theirs?' That way the work gets done and everything's a whole lot less complicated. Besides, weren't we all hired for the same reason? For our technical expertise?"

"You were hired to *produce results* for UGAT. And throughout your career many of the results you'll be required to produce will be with and through other people—either as a team member, part of a network, or perhaps later on as a leader."

Both sat in silence as Albert thought for a moment about what Megan had just said.

"These weren't the things we talked about when you hired me."

Megan raised an eyebrow and sat back in her chair. "You're right, Albert. But at that time there wasn't much to talk about. All your achievements throughout your educational career you accomplished by yourself. And they were exceptional, no doubt about it. Exceptional enough to cause me to hire you on the basis of those achievements and hope you'd either have, or be able to develop, the networking and peer influence skills you'll need in order to have a successful career with UGAT—or anywhere else you might work for that matter."

"Networking skills?"

"Not like computer networks or systems, Albert. I'm talking about people skills—the ability to work with others to produce meaningful results."

"What if I'm one of those who is better off working alone?"

"You may be. There will always be roles for individual contributors. But those roles are scarce—and they are becoming fewer and fewer. And even if you find one of those roles, you'll still have to get along with others to be effective."

Albert felt trapped. He didn't like what he had heard. He didn't like his options. He felt alone in a hostile world.

After a few moments, Megan continued. "I know this probably makes you feel uncomfortable. But don't feel alone, Albert. You're not the only one who has to face this reality."

Albert sat there in silence. He didn't know what to say. If what she said was true—that he needed to work well with people to produce better results—then he was in trouble. He could feel the knot in his stomach begin to form again. He had taken a couple of interpersonal communications courses, and none of what he had learned ever worked for him.

Megan went on. "If there's one thing we really don't teach people these days, it's how to produce results by working well with others. Our schools try to teach people how to talk and listen, to learn and grow with others, but most of their efforts miss the mark. And it's a huge challenge for us here at UGAT and throughout the industry. I'm sure it's a problem in other industries as well. But that's the reason we recruit so heavily from UNM."

"What do you mean?" asked Albert.

"Well, if you want to know the truth, I'm surprised that you're challenged by all this. Because most people who graduate from UNM have picked up at least some of the Coach's winning ways."

"Coach who? And *what* winning ways?"

"Coach Calvert."

"Wasn't he the football coach?"

"Still is the football coach."

"Was he a professor or something, too?" asked Albert.

"No. He's just the football coach—but has been for twenty-two years."

"Yeah, I heard something about that. Set some kind of record, too, didn't he?"

Megan shook her head in disbelief. "Only the best

record in the history of all of college football. A record that everyone says will never be broken. Ever. Two hundred and thirty-nine wins against three losses. But the losses were a long time ago."

"Yeah, but give me a break. We're talking UNM—University of Northeastern Michigan—not Notre Dame or Nebraska or something. It isn't Division I. It's Division IIA or something like that. They don't even play in a real stadium, with stands and stuff."

"No, but the teams they play are real. And those teams want to beat UNM. Some are really good teams—and besides, they're all in our league, so someone must think they're competitive. And they are. We play teams from schools just like ours."

"Something must be different," observed Albert.

"Something is different," responded Megan. "The Coach."

Albert sat there, taking this all in, wondering where it was leading.

"I'm amazed," continued Megan, "that someone as bright as you could have graduated from UNM knowing so little about the Coach and his football legacy. But it does explain why you know so little about his winning ways."

Albert thought about this for a moment. "You talk about the Coach's winning ways almost as though they were some kind of religion or mantra—something sacred or special like that. Is it formalized or something?" Then, thinking he might as well get to his real concern: "And how does all this football stuff relate to me?"

Albert's question caused Megan to ease up somewhat. She realized that there may be hope for him yet. *Amazing what a little conversation, however challenging, can do for a person's attitude,* she thought.

"First off, let's get one thing straight. It's not the football stuff that matters," Megan explained.

"Then what is it?" asked Albert.

"What's important is what Coach does to produce the results he does with his teams. Or better yet, what his players learn from him that helps his teams produce the results they do."

"Is this going to be about teambuilding? There was some of that in one of those courses I took."

"Maybe some of it. Any time a team does well you can rest assured the principles of teamwork are in action. But it's way, way more than that."

"Like what?"

Megan was starting to feel like she was making at least a little headway with Albert. "Way more than we can talk about here. You've got some major learning ahead of you, Albert. It's going to take a lot of work."

"But why should I bother? I don't like football, I don't like teams—especially these Tiger Teams we have around here—and I work better alone."

Megan looked Albert straight in the eye and said, "I'll accept the fact that you don't like football and I can see that you don't like teams. But Albert, your last comment is dead wrong. You don't work better alone."

"What?" Albert was startled.

"You don't work better alone."

"I thought that was the whole reason we're having this conversation. The team didn't like me. I didn't like them. I do better on my own."

"You're right. Things didn't go well with the team. I don't know if it's fair to say they didn't like you, but it is clear that things didn't work as well as they should."

"And I do better on my own," Albert declared.

"That's where you're wrong."

"What are you saying? That you don't like the work I do on my own, either?"

"I'm not saying that. I'm saying that we don't agree on what 'better' means."

"I don't get it." Albert was getting tense again.

"You say you work better on your own. I'm saying that it all depends on what 'better' means. Better according to what criteria? Better according to whose standards?"

"That's simple," responded Albert. "Better according to what the work is and how well it's done."

"So better means quality of work?"

"What other criteria are there?"

"Let's use an example. Let's say a customer has a problem that requires a technical solution. I ask you to solve it. You spend three weeks and $50,000 to develop the highest quality solution possible. Let's say your solution wins design awards, is worthy of publication in technical journals, and even contains new technology that UGAT can patent so we can reap huge financial rewards in the future."

"Sounds good," said Albert, clearly relishing the thought of himself being in that position.

"However," Megan went on, "let's say the customer needed a quick fix, help in a couple of days. Assume the customer also wasn't planning on spending more than $5,000, and didn't give a hoot whether it was new technology, old technology, or a bunch of rubber bands that solved the problem, as long as the solution allowed operational needs to be met."

"But that's different," countered Albert.

"The only thing different is perspective," explained Megan. "Quality is relative. It's multifaceted. And it takes into account a number of factors other than simple technical merit."

"So what's your point?"

"Even technical merit isn't as objective as you'd like to make it, Albert. In today's corporate environment, technical merit is as subjective as the term 'quality' often is."

"So?"

"So that's why teams are important. That's why working well with others, inside or outside of teams, is important.

That's why learning to produce results with others is important. And, in a nutshell, that's why what Coach teaches is important. It's the way he teaches his players to work well with others to produce better results that's so useful."

"How do you know so much about him and his teams?" Albert slipped back into his reluctant inquiry mode.

"I was one of the team's student trainers for my last three years at UNM. I figured if he could win so many games over the years, there must be some secret to his success. The best way to find out the secret was to get close. For me, the best way to get close was to be part of it. Being a student trainer was one of the most rewarding experiences of my life."

"So what's his secret?" Albert had a knack for getting to the point.

"It's not that simple," answered Megan, "and if you really want to learn, if you're really serious about using his philosophies and ideas, the best way to learn is from Coach himself."

"I'm not sure I want to go back to school. Football isn't my thing, and a lot of that stuff doesn't work for people like me. And it's too late to learn from him because I've already graduated. So can't you just tell me and we'll see what happens?"

"Sorry," Megan answered. "I think in this case it's best you learn from the Coach. I'll help you, but it'll be better if you work with the master himself. But before either of us invests any energy into helping you learn the winning ways, we first need to make sure that you believe it will make a difference in your life."

"I won't know whether they will make a difference until I know what they are," explained Albert.

"That's a problem," responded Megan, "because if you aren't convinced of the importance of these principles, then you'll never learn them in the right way."

"You see, Albert," Megan continued, "it's not just knowing about the winning ways that's important—it's about living according to the principles. It's about internalizing the concepts so they become part of you and you live your life that way every single moment in everything you do."

Albert just sat there with a blank look on his face.

"I think we've gone far enough for today," declared Megan. "Let's get together this coming Friday and decide what our next step will be. Meantime, during the week I have an assignment for you to complete."

"Assignment?" asked Albert, somewhat hesitantly.

"I want you to talk to some people, ask them a few questions, and see what you learn."

"Who?" asked Albert, even more hesitantly. He didn't want to go back to the members of the infamous Tiger Team.

"A variety of people chosen from a few lists I'll give you," explained Megan. "Here. Write these down as I explain the various groups I want you to choose from." She handed him a yellow writing pad and a pencil.

"The first group consists of UNM graduates who work for UGAT. I'll e-mail you a list of their names and extension numbers. It includes the President, and I'd like him to be one of the people you talk to."

Albert looked up in surprise.

Megan continued. "The second group is about a dozen UNM graduates who are leaders in our industry and who don't work for UGAT.

"The third group is composed of tenured professors in the computer science department and career counselors from UNM. The fourth group to choose from is made up of officers and committee chairpersons of the computer science professional organization—many of the preeminent leaders in our field. And finally, there's a half dozen head hunters we use from time to time to help find highly skilled people we need. And you're free to add to the list anyone you think might be beneficial.

"I want you to call and talk to at least two people from each group. Ask each person the following three questions.

"The first question is: What career paths and opportunities exist in our field for someone who wants to work alone and can't work with groups or other people?

"Question number two is: Of all the skills and abilities

you can think of, what are the most important for someone to develop in order to be successful in our field?

"The final question is: When people in our field fail, what shortcomings or skill deficiencies most contributed to their failure?

"Listen to their responses, take good notes, and summarize the key points in their answers in a matrix so you can see what patterns exist in their thinking. Then you and I can discuss the results next week. Any questions?" Megan looked at Albert as he finished writing the last question on his yellow pad.

Deep down inside, Albert had become intrigued with the idea of this project. It would be interesting to see how his beliefs measured up against Megan's. He was somewhat optimistic that the conversations would give him enough information that he could use to convince her to let him do his own thing. Indeed, he felt confident that some of the more credible people on the list would support his position. They would say that people who share Albert's abilities and potential would be able to succeed on their own with the right kind of freedom and support.

The more he thought about it, the more he looked forward to the project. And besides, he liked the logic of the matrix.

He scribbled a matrix with four columns across a blank yellow page and turned it toward Megan. "I'll list the names of people I call down the left-hand side, and reserve one column for each of the questions. I'll take notes separately, but I'll summarize the two or three key points from each answer in each cell."

"Perfect," declared Megan. "I'll e-mail the lists right away, and see you next week, same time."

Albert plopped down in front of his computer and immediately began constructing his matrix on a spreadsheet so he could summarize the results of his phone interviews.

In a short time he finished the matrix, then went into his electronic mailbox. Sure enough, the lists Megan had promised were all attached to a short note wishing him well on his assignment.

Albert began calling right away. Rather than just call a couple of people from each list, however, he decided to call each and every one and see if he could actually make voice-to-voice contact with them all before the week was out.

With each passing day it became more obvious that the results weren't turning out the way Albert expected. At first he thought he had just hit a few people whose perspectives were off the mark. He was glad he had already decided to call everyone on each list. But as he got deeper and deeper into each list, the patterns held strong and the answers remained consistent.

The more calls he made, the more upset he became. At

first he went into denial. Next he got angry. Then he became depressed. He couldn't sleep at night. He was constantly tense and on edge. He was just plain miserable.

Albert tried to rationalize the data he was collecting. *Something was wrong with the questions. Maybe because he didn't know most of the people that well, they weren't really leveling with him. Maybe he was misunderstanding their answers.* The misery persisted.

Nonetheless, Albert dutifully carried out his assignment. By the end of the week, he was a basket case.

The results of his research were clear, but they didn't fit with Albert's beliefs about performance, achievement, fulfillment, satisfaction, or anything else about career success. *They had to be wrong. This was some kind of bad joke. Or maybe a conspiracy to get even with him for losing his cool with the Tiger Team.* There just had to be some explanation other than the fact that he had completely missed the boat about all this.

What about everything else I believe? he asked himself. *Is everything I hold true just as far off from what other people believe?* Albert was shaken to the core. He was even more shaken when he realized he didn't have a clue what to do about it.

Albert showed up late for his next meeting with Megan.

His appearance was disheveled, and he seemed to be somewhat distracted.

Megan spoke first. "Good morning, Albert. How'd it go?"

"Morning." Albert wasn't exactly in a talkative mood.

"Do you want a cup of coffee or something, Albert? You look like you haven't quite awakened yet this morning."

"No, I already had some. Thanks."

"Well, how'd it go?"

After a short pause, Albert responded: "I'm not sure what you wanted me to find out."

"From the questions?" asked Megan. "Did you call at least two people from each list?"

"I called everyone on all the lists."

"Everyone?"

"Everyone. I connected with all but four of them."

"That's quite a few people, Albert. You must have spent most of your time on the phone this past week."

"Almost all of it. Morning, noon, and even at night."

"So, what did you find out?"

"What did you want me to find out? Did you e-mail them first or something?"

"I simply wanted you to find out the truth. No, I didn't e-mail them or talk to them first. But it sounds like maybe there were some consistencies in what they had to say."

"You might say that." Albert wasn't exactly diving into this conversation with gusto.

"So what did they say?" Megan persisted.

"Very few. Ability to get along well with others. Lack of ability to get along with others."

"What?"

"Very few. Ability to get along. Lack of ability to get along. Are those the answers you're looking for?"

"I'm not sure I'm with you," responded Megan.

"Question number one: What career paths and opportunities exist in our field for someone who wants to work alone and can't work with groups or other people? Answer number one: very few.

"Question number two: Of all the skills and abilities you can think of, what are the most important for someone to develop in order to be successful in our field? Answer number two: ability to get along well with others.

"Question number three: When people in our field fail, what shortcomings or skill deficiencies most contributed to their failure? Answer number three: lack of ability to get along with others."

"Oh, I'm with you now. Well, what do you think?"

"I think it's a setup."

"A setup?" Megan asked. "Why?"

"Because everyone knows nothing would ever get designed, developed, or produced and delivered without technical expertise, and not one of them said it was most important."

"Did you ask any of them why they didn't say it was important?" Megan queried.

"Yes, a few of them."

"And?"

"They said technical expertise was important, but not nearly as important as being able to use your expertise to work with others. They talked about peer leadership, positive peer influence, network leadership, and stuff like that, and said all that stuff was way more important. To quote one esteemed source, 'the image of the individual contributor as a superstar is a myth of a bygone era.' They said expertise only matters if you can combine it with that of your co-workers."

"Do you believe them?"

"They all had examples. Lots of them."

"Do you believe them?" Megan pressed.

"I was surprised at how much they agreed."

"I'll bet. Do you believe them?"

There was a long silence. Megan let the silence work. After a few moments that seemed to each like an eternity, Albert started shaking—first his hands, then his whole body. Then tears welled up in his eyes and started streaming down his cheeks. He lowered his head into his hands, silently sobbing as he quickly arose from his chair and left Megan's office.

Megan waited about an hour before going to see Albert in his office. He was at the computer, one hand on the keyboard, the other on his mouse.

Megan sat down in the chair next to his desk without saying anything.

Albert continued to dawdle on his computer.

Albert finally spoke first. "Can I help you?"

"We didn't finish our conversation."

"You win. I got the point," he said as he continued to focus on the computer screen.

"I'm not so sure."

"What did I miss?" he asked. It was obvious he was still feeling a great deal of pain.

"Albert, the last thing I want to do is upset you. But I do want to make sure we do the right thing. We need to make sure we take advantage of what we've learned."

"What *we've* learned? Or what *I've* learned?"

"Both, Albert. I'm on your side. This isn't me against you. It isn't *anybody* against you. I want you to succeed and find fulfillment. So does everyone else."

Silence again settled in as Albert continued to work on his computer.

This time Megan broke the silence. "The answer isn't in your computer, Albert."

"Where is it then?"

"You tell me."

Again, silence, broken only by the occasional clicks emanating from Albert's mouse.

Once again Megan took the initiative. "Albert, the answer has to come from you."

"I don't want to go to another training program. I hated those kinds of classes and they obviously didn't get their point across to me anyway."

"What if you went back to school, but in a different way?"

"Like what?"

"What if you just went back for a few visits? Spent some time with Coach, one-on-one, and picked his brain by yourself?"

"Me? Spending one-on-one time with a football coach? He's used to working with jocks. He wouldn't give me the time of day."

"He did me. Do I look like a jock?"

"You're different. Besides, you worked for him."

"Some day I'd be interested in knowing what you mean by 'different,' but the fact is, I'm not different. He spent time with me because I wanted to learn about the things he taught his teams. He never runs out of time for people who want to learn the secrets of his winning ways. But this is a pointless argument, because I've already spoken with him. Twice. And he said he'd be happy to spend time with you. But only if you are ready to change and willing to try the things he suggests. He doesn't have time if all you're going to do is talk."

Albert silently stared at his computer screen.

Finally he spoke. "I guess I'll give it a try."

Megan rose up from her chair. "Coach says trying is

just a noisy way of not doing something, Albert. That won't be good enough. Either you decide you're going to do it, or you decide you're not. But your commitment has to be total. It'll still be hard enough even if you want to do it right with your whole heart and soul. It'll be impossible if you're only committed partway."

As she headed for the door, she concluded the conversation by saying, "Albert, today's Friday. Think about all this over the weekend and come see me Monday morning. If you're totally committed to work with Coach, I'll set it up immediately. Fall practice starts in two weeks so we can arrange for you to get involved then. If you're commitment isn't total, then we'll look at other options. But let's be honest with each other about this so we don't waste our time or the Coach's."

Megan left Albert alone with his computer.

The digital clock radio next to Albert's bed read 3:14 on Saturday morning when it all came together for Albert. He wasn't sure what exactly happened, but at that moment he sat up in bed and knew that he should work with Coach Calvert.

Albert didn't even know why, but the decision felt right and brought a great deal of comfort and joy. The tension and pressure he had felt for the past few weeks dissipated, and a great burden lifted from his shoulders. He almost felt carefree—a feeling he hadn't felt in years. In fact he couldn't remember the last time he had felt quite this good about life in general and the rest of the world.

He tried to go back to sleep, but couldn't. His energy level was just too high. So at the crack of dawn, he threw a towel, swimsuit, and a bunch of junk into the back of his Saturn. He packed a bowl, some food, and water for Digger and the two headed for the shore.

Albert ran up and down the beach with Digger, playing and frolicking in the water. They played Frisbee in the waves until they were exhausted. They watched little kids build sand castles. It was a great day. That night he slept like a baby.

On Sunday, Albert awakened just in time to make it to morning worship services—something he hadn't done in quite a while.

Later that morning he took Digger for a walk. Then he went to a baseball game at Wrigley Field. He arrived at the ticket window just as they were releasing some of the unused scout tickets, so Albert got a seat right behind home plate in row twenty. The crowd seemed especially warm and friendly, it was an exciting game, and the Cubs won in the bottom of the ninth.

When he got home, he took Digger for another walk. Then he went to bed Sunday night as pleasantly tired as he had been on Saturday night. He fell asleep wondering what Monday would bring.

Albert walked into Megan's office right on time.

"Good morning, Albert," she smiled as she looked up from the stack of papers in front of her.

"When do I start with the Coach?" asked Albert.

"It sounds like you've made up your mind."

"Let's get it over with," Albert responded.

"This isn't like going to the dentist, Albert. It's not like working with Coach is something you survive," explained Megan.

"Whatever," said Albert. Now that he had made his decision and had this newfound energy, he was eager to finish his "lessons" and get back to his real work.

"Learning about people shouldn't be seen as skimming through one small section in one chapter of the Book of Life, Albert. If you truly want to be effective with people and to learn how to work with others to achieve exciting things in life, then your learning must be a lifelong quest. Working with Coach and learning the winning ways is only the first step in that lifelong journey."

"I'm sorry. I am serious about this. I guess what I meant is let's get this first step going and see what happens."

"I appreciate your enthusiasm, Albert. And I'm glad that you've decided to move forward. I've already arranged for you to meet with Coach next Monday at 8:00 A.M. in his office on campus. He's looking forward to meeting you. I've arranged for this to be part of your development plan for the year, so whatever time you and Coach spend together, you can charge to training. I'd like a report from you every two weeks and Coach said he'd give me a call every couple of weeks as well. Any questions?"

"Nope."

"That's it, then. I'll look forward to hearing from you in about three weeks."

"Okay," responded Albert as he left Megan's office.

The week passed by in a hurry with Albert working diligently on his projects while at the same time using every spare moment to think about what his sessions with the Coach would be like.

On Monday morning he had awakened at 4:00 so he could get a good start for the three-hour drive and would arrive at Coach's office with a little time to spare. The last thing he wanted to do was show up late for their first meeting.

Albert reached the UNM campus at 7:25. He stopped at the Student Union Center for a quick bite of breakfast before walking over to the Coach's office. After only a slight hesitation, he knocked on the Coach's door at 7:58.

"Come on in," responded Coach from behind the door.

Albert looked around as he entered. The office was about twelve feet wide and twelve feet deep. The back wall comprised four sections of floor-to-ceiling bookcases. A few of the shelves had books, but most were cluttered with pictures, souvenirs, and other football memorabilia. An old oak desk provided the foundation for the Coach's work station. It was butted against the wall on the left side of the room, so when the Coach worked at the desk he faced the wall. That placed the Coach's chair right in front of the door. He swiveled in his chair and rose to face Albert, as Albert stepped through the door.

"You must be the rising star Megan told me about. Well, you're right on time."

Rising star? thought Albert. *He's got me mixed up with someone else.*

"Just call me Coach," he said, extending his arm for a handshake. "Everyone else does."

"Okay, Coach. Uh, I'm Albert, Albert Garroway," Albert responded as he shook the Coach's hand.

Pleasant handshake, reflected Albert. *Not one of those crushing ones like you might expect from someone who spent a lot of time around jocks.* He hadn't known what the Coach would look like, but Albert relaxed as soon as he saw him. He was average height, with a UNM ball cap tilted back on his head. A few too many helpings of everything made it a stretch for his cardigan sweater to wrap around the bulge of his middle-aged midriff. His crumpled trousers almost matched the plaid, button-down shirt he was wearing. His pleasant, round face provided a comfortable setting for two eyes that literally twinkled their delight at meeting someone new. *He could pass for anybody's favorite uncle,* thought Albert.

"Have a seat, Albert," said the Coach, gesturing to the chair next to his desk. "Care for some coffee or something?"

"No, thanks, I just had breakfast."

The Coach sat back down in his chair. Albert noticed that both chairs were identical—oak swivel chairs with leather padded seats. *Did he purposefully keep the chairs the same?* Albert asked himself.

"Did you drive up this morning?" asked the Coach.

"Yeah, it took a little under two hours."

"We could have furnished you a room last night."

"That's what Megan said. But I usually get up early anyway and the drive was okay."

"Well, whenever you want to come up early we can get you a room."

"Thanks."

"Well, then. What are we gonna do?"

"What do you mean?" asked Albert. *Is this some kind of setup?* he thought to himself. *Maybe this wasn't such a great idea.*

"I mean why did you want to come see me?"

"Didn't Megan tell you?"

"She told me you are one of the most talented people in the organization. And she said based on some discussions she'd had with you, she thought you'd like to spend some time with me to pick up on a few things you felt you'd missed during your time here. I said I'd do whatever I can. And here we are."

"That's all she said?" asked Albert.

"That's pretty much it."

"What she and I talked about a little was the way you have with people. But she really didn't say much, other than you taught her a lot about it and she thought you could help me." Albert was uncomfortable. *Why doesn't he just tell me what I need to know and let me get on with it?* he thought.

"I'm going to need some help from you to determine how I can best respond to your needs, Albert," Coach explained. "Whatever information I can share will only be useful if it's important to you. So let's take a few minutes to talk about what you'd like to get out of the time we spend together."

"I guess I need to learn how to get along with other people," offered Albert.

"You seem pleasant enough to me."

"It's more than just getting along. It's working with other people—getting them to accept my ideas and really being able to influence them," explained Albert.

"Is that all?"

"For me that seems to be enough, at least for starters. It's working on teams that started it."

"Working on teams?"

"Or maybe *not* working on teams," Albert said as he

managed a laugh. "But then I got to thinking. I don't really work well with anyone—at least not like most other people do. Most people seem to enjoy working with others, but it always seems to not work out too well for me."

"I think most people would like to be more effective in their dealings with other people."

"Really?"

"Really. Almost everyone knows that the number one common fear is speaking in front of a large group. But what we lose sight of is that the second fear most people share is that of their own shyness."

"Most people are worried about being shy?" asked Albert.

"That's right. And over half are worried to the point that they fear their shyness might be a serious personality defect."

"I didn't know that," declared Albert.

"Most people don't," explained the Coach. "But almost everyone wishes he or she could do better in their dealings with other people."

"I guess deep down inside that's something I've always wanted, too," said Albert. "Although I've hated to admit it—even to myself."

"Well, if that's why you're here, we're in luck, because I have picked up a few ideas along the way that can probably be of some help."

"I can't wait," said Albert, and for the first time in as long as he could remember, he wasn't being sarcastic when he used those words.

"Good," responded the Coach. He was growing to like Albert already. "Then here's how we'll do it. Over the years I've learned a few principles that can make a huge difference. They're more than just principles for getting along with people. I like to think they're principles for making good things happen."

"I like it already," interjected Albert.

"Some people call them Coach's secrets, although I've never tried to conceal them from anyone. Others call them the secrets of winning ways. I guess it's okay to call them secrets, because they are like secrets to a person until that person is ready to open his or her mind to their true meaning. Unless you're truly willing to accept their power and live your life in accordance with their meaning, they'll remain secrets to you, too. You'll hear them, but never understand how to use them."

"I'm ready," said Albert.

"Good. Let's start you off by sharing the principle of giving power away."

"Giving power away?" asked Albert.

"Yes. It's the first secret. The more power you give, the more you get," responded the Coach.

"I don't understand," said Albert.

"Most people think of power in terms of formal authority, position, status, things like that. Words they associate with power are words like control, command, coerce, dominate, govern, or manipulate. Certainly, there's that side of things. But there's also a flip side."

"Which is?"

"Power as a positive force. Power used to build people up. The kind of power we use to guide, facilitate, motivate, and energize. The kind of power that causes others to feel stronger rather than weaker as a result of my interactions with them."

Albert was almost mesmerized by what he was hearing. The Coach continued.

"People who rely on negative, coercive power try to get all they can, usually by making others feel weaker. They fight for positional authority. They fight for status. They fight to keep others from getting power, because they think the more power others have, the less powerful they themselves will be. The problem with that in today's world is that people don't respond to this kind of power like they used to. Formal authority as a source of power has eroded.

"Conversely, people who rely on positive power try to give as much away as they can. They believe that the stronger they make the people around them, the stronger they will become. For example, that was the magic behind John

Kennedy's charisma. When people heard him speak, not only did they feel better about him, they felt better about themselves. They felt stronger and more powerful as individuals. The key to his impact was the power he gave to others.

"So now you know the first secret: **Make Others Feel Stronger Rather than Weaker** as a result of your interactions with them."

"Sounds like some kind of manipulation to me," declared Albert.

"If you use any of the secrets to merely manipulate people, that's just what they'll be—*manipulations*—and sooner rather than later the people you try to manipulate will realize what's happening and you'll be much worse off for having tried."

"But all this psychological stuff has always seemed liked nothing but manipulations to me," said Albert. *I hope he doesn't think I'm trying to be difficult,* he thought.

"I appreciate your honesty and your skepticism, Albert. But I'm talking about a principle here—a goal to strive for in all your interactions. It's not a specific thing you say; it's a completely different way to look at things and to frame your interactions with people."

"So if I change the way I think about interacting with people, my behavior will follow and hopefully it won't seem like I'm trying to be manipulative."

"It won't seem like you're trying to be manipulative," said the Coach, "because you *won't* be manipulative."

"So tell me what making other people feel powerful means," said Albert.

"For starters it means recognizing their intelligence, their ideas, their effort, and their contribution. It means respecting them and respecting what they've done."

"What do I do if what they've done isn't as good as what I've done?" asked Albert.

"It doesn't have to be as good as your work for it to be worthwhile. It probably isn't as good as they could do either, if given a chance to do better. But it should be valued and respected based on the effort they've put into it. If you respect them and their effort, you'll have a much better opportunity to inspire them to greater performance and to allow you to help them achieve it."

"I guess that makes sense," Albert observed.

"Most people try to establish a pecking order when they form relationships with others. Usually they want to be on top—to be superior in the order. You don't need to be on top to be effective. In fact, the more on top you are, the more likely you are to fall down, because no one else will want to stay on the bottom for too long."

"But someone has to be on top and that means someone has to be on the bottom," countered Albert.

"Not necessarily. Why can't you show *equal* respect for each other?"

"Even if your abilities aren't equal?" asked Albert. "That doesn't seem honest."

"No two people will ever have exactly equal abilities. But that's not what we're talking about. We're talking about respect for each other as people, respect for the abilities people do possess, and respect for their efforts. One of the worst habits a person can develop is to constantly compare his or her abilities and efforts to those of everyone else and vice versa."

"But if you're working together, how can you avoid comparisons?" asked Albert.

"First, by recognizing that there will always be differences, both in people and the way they perform. Second, by involving others in your thinking and decision making. These are the most important principles I use in building winning football teams every year."

"How's that?" Albert was hooked.

"Our competitors think we win because we have a fantastic playbook and incredible game plans. Our playbook *is* pretty solid and our game plans well formulated. But it's not the plays that win games for us; *it's the players!*"

"But everybody could say that," countered Albert.

"Most people *do* say it," agreed Coach. "But that doesn't mean they know what it means and act in accordance with the true meaning."

"What do you mean?" asked Albert.

"All our players have strengths and weaknesses. I guess

you could also say that means that some are better than others. But it's not better or worse that matters. The important thing is to accept that they are different and build a game plan around the things each does well, without letting their weaknesses undermine the team's efforts."

Albert listened intently. These were things he had never thought of before.

"Too many coaches spend too much time trying to identify their players' weaknesses and develop them so the players will fit their game plan. I only have one season with each team—ten games. So I don't have much time. I've found it much better to build on the different mix of strengths each group brings to the team each year than to try and overcome all their weaknesses. And the important thing is that they feel better about the team and themselves, so they work harder to develop the strengths they have."

It's probably not much different than our Tiger Teams, thought Albert.

"But it's also important to involve them in the discussions and decision making. I respect their insights and opinions. Often during a game when something's not working, the best thing I can do is ask the player what's happening. Almost always we can work together to come up with something that will work while making better use of the player's strengths."

"But you're in charge," observed Albert. "So if you disagree, you can always do what you want anyway."

"That's right. But it doesn't do any good to do what I want to do if we don't win. And the only way we can win is for everyone to really be in touch with each other, knowing their strengths, respecting their efforts, and helping every single person on the team achieve their best. You see, Albert, it's not just me who helps them. They all help each other just as much."

"So the way they communicate with each other is as important as the way you communicate with them."

"More important. How well do you think you communicate with Megan?" asked the coach.

"Okay, I guess," answered Albert.

"How well do you communicate with your peers?"

"Not so well."

"And, why do you think you're here?"

"Because Megan thinks it's important for me to be able to communicate and work better with other people," answered Albert.

"Megan does? Or *you* do?"

"I guess *I* do," admitted Albert. "Especially after all the people I've talked to during the past couple of weeks."

"So tell me what you think will be most helpful about the things we've discussed today." Coach leaned back in his chair, ready to listen.

"It's important for me to make the people I work with feel more powerful rather than less powerful as a result of my interactions with them."

"Well said." Coach was truly pleased.

"But wait a minute," interjected Albert. "If that's all I focus on, how will they see my strengths or recognize all the good work I've done?"

"Has anyone besides Megan seen or recognized any of these things so far?"

"Not really," answered Albert.

"And the odds are that they never will if you continue the way I suspect you've been operating. Once you show them the respect they deserve, then the respect you deserve will come its way."

"Then I guess I've got nothing to lose by trying it."

But Coach wasn't finished. "How are you going to try to help people feel stronger rather than weaker?"

"By finding their strengths, recognizing what they have to offer, and honoring their efforts. And by asking their opinions—getting them involved and treating them as peers."

"Excellent!" Coach knew it wouldn't be as easy to apply as Albert was anticipating, but he was pleased that Albert had at least picked up the essence of this first principle so quickly.

They agreed to meet again during one of the team's practices in a couple of weeks and Albert headed home.

During his drive home, Albert thought a lot about his newly acquired knowledge and about Coach.

If he makes everyone he deals with feel as good as he made me feel today, he's pretty good, thought Albert. He recalled meetings he'd had with other people to whom he had gone for help. More often than not, they made him feel stupid or inadequate. Some lectured. Some patronized him. All in all, those experiences left a bad taste in his mouth.

But his experience with Coach was different from the beginning. *He made me feel good about him and about myself from the moment we met,* reflected Albert. *And he never once talked about my problem as though something was wrong with me. In fact, I don't remember him even talking about my problem at all. He didn't talk about himself, either. But he still gave me a ton to work on, and it all seems to fit together. Interesting. No—more than interesting; all this is pretty incredible.*

Albert's mind was still spinning with all these thoughts when he returned to his office that afternoon. Fortunately, Megan was away somewhere at a meeting so he didn't have to explain anything to her. *I can use some time to collect my thoughts,* thought Albert.

He decided that if he was going to make this journey a meaningful one, it would be best if he kept a journal. So he decided to start an electronic journal on his computer. In it he typed:

Secret of Winning Ways:

Make People Feel Stronger Rather than Weaker as a result of your interactions with them.

Then he typed:

• *Forget about pecking orders of any type.* This includes organizational as well as intellectual hierarchies.

• *Recognize people's strengths.* Focus on what people bring to the party, not what they leave home.

• *Honor people's efforts.* Build upon the things that other people have achieved, not what they haven't.

• *Involve others in planning, problem solving, and decision making.* Work with people rather than against them, with the knowledge that more can be accomplished through collaboration than competition.

Then it occurred to Albert that it might be helpful to include a few ideas about what the first secret was *not*. So he also typed the following:

Make People Feel Stronger Rather than Weaker as a result of my interactions with them does *not* mean:

• Using idle flattery in an attempt to win their approval.

• Offering help in ways that cause people to feel inferior.

• Giving up my own self-esteem.

Albert then programmed his computer so the first secret would prop on his screen each morning when he turned it on.

As Albert went about his business for the next couple of weeks he tried diligently—but carefully—to find ways to use what he had learned from Coach. He was especially careful because he didn't want anyone to jump to the conclusion that he was trying out the latest craze in pop psychology. And even though everything Coach said made sense, he wasn't sure it would work. *After all, if it worked that well, why didn't everyone know about it and use it?*

However, he didn't let his skepticism prevail. He just put into practice his newly gained knowledge, and when he wasn't in a position to use it, he just kept quiet or stayed out of people's way.

To his satisfaction, it worked. It didn't produce any earthshaking, hugely revolutionary results, but it worked. Every time he tried to act in accordance with the principle he had learned from Coach, the results were positive. People responded positively, with none of the hostility and reserve he had always experienced in the past.

In fact, the results were so consistently positive that one night Albert lay awake wondering if it all wasn't part of some big conspiracy. He finally concluded that it would be too hard to orchestrate a conspiracy of that magnitude, especially since so many of the opportunities to test the principle had occurred almost happenstance in the normal course of business. *No,* he finally concluded, *the only logical conclusion is that the principle works.*

The next day was his scheduled update with Megan. Albert showed up at the appointed hour.

"Good morning, Albert. You're looking relaxed and refreshed."

"Thanks. Yeah, I feel pretty good. You're right about Coach; he's an interesting dude."

"I'm glad you like him. I spoke with Richard this morning and he said things are going better with the Tiger Team."

"We've still got a lot of work to do."

"I realize the project has a long way to go. But he said you seem to have taken a different approach with the other team members and everyone feels better about it."

"Really?"

"Naturally there's some skepticism. It'll take a while for some people to conclude that this is the real you. But for the most part, everyone's reaction is positive. How do you like it?"

"Okay, I guess. I have to be honest, none of this seems normal to me," explained Albert.

"It'll take a while to develop a new comfort zone, even though this is a better way to do things. Sometimes our old habits tend to stick with us even if they're wrong just because we're comfortable with them."

"Has Coach always been this way?" asked Albert.

"As far as I know."

"It doesn't make sense. I mean that he could come from football and be a coach and all, and think this way."

"I think the lesson is that this isn't about football, Albert. It's about life and about being a winner."

"Well I've still got a lot to learn," said Albert as he rose from his chair and left Megan's office, deep in thought.

Albert showed up at the football team's practice field exactly on time for his next appointed meeting with Coach.

During the team's warm-up exercises, Coach walked over to greet Albert on the sidelines.

"How are you doing, Albert? Good to see you again."

"Hi, Coach. I'm doing fine. Are you sure this is a good time for you? You've got a lot to do."

"Are you pressed for time?" the Coach asked Albert.

"I'm fine," responded Albert.

"Good. Then what I want you to do is just watch. Observe. Pay attention to everything you see during this practice. After it's over, we'll talk about what you've seen. Okay?"

"Sure," agreed Albert. He'd never watched a football practice before. And although he wasn't sure whether it would be interesting, at least it would be different. There was something to be said for new experiences.

So Albert watched everything that happened during practice. Or at least he tried to watch everything.

The first thing that occurred to him was that there was a lot going on all the time. After about fifteen minutes of warm-up exercises, one of the equipment managers sounded a blast on an air horn and everyone jogged to a particular place on the field. Albert counted eight different locations where various-sized groups of coaches and players gathered. Each group immediately started performing different exercises.

Albert quickly surmised that the groups were formed based on the players' positions. The groups worked through a series of maneuvers until another blast on the air horn sounded twenty minutes later.

At the sound of the second blast everyone jogged to new groups. They worked another twenty minutes until the air horn blasted again.

All the offensive players gathered at one end of the field while the defensive players hustled to the other. They again went through the same type of drills. When the air horn sounded at the end of twenty minutes, each group jogged to the goalpost at their respective end of the field.

Albert walked to the end of the field where the offensive team had gathered on one knee around the offensive coaching staff, just as one of the coaches began to speak.

"That's pretty much the complete game plan for this week. Tell us where you think we might have problems and ways you think we can improve it."

Albert listened in fascination as the group discussed different changes they could make and improvements they could implement based on what they knew about each other's abilities and their overall capability as a team. After another twenty minutes, the air horn sounded again and the two units went back onto the field to implement these changes.

The two units drilled for another half an hour until a final blast from the air horn signaled the end of practice. As the players jogged from the field, Coach joined Albert on the sideline.

"Well, Albert, what do you think?"

"It's way more organized than I ever imagined it would be," said Albert.

"Sometimes we don't think it's all that organized, but today wasn't too bad. It does take a lot to get everyone working together in such a short amount of time each week."

"I can imagine," observed Albert.

"And they all have different strengths and weaknesses and each plays a different role on the team," explained the Coach.

"I think I'm about to learn another secret, and I don't think it's about organization," offered Albert.

"Right," Coach agreed. "The organizational part is reasonably straightforward, although I have to admit, a lot of people don't get it. The second secret is about camels."

"What?" asked Albert.

"Camels," stated the Coach. "Here's one for you, Albert. Just what are camels?"

"Horses put together by a committee?" responded Albert with a bit of a grin.

"I figured you'd have heard that one," said the Coach. "Are camels good or bad?"

"Mostly bad," said Albert. "That's the point of the joke."

"Well, the joke is wrong," countered the Coach. **"Camels are okay. That's the second secret."**

"Camels are okay?" asked Albert.

"Camels are not only okay; they're necessary. Think about what you just saw."

"You mean the organization."

"No, that was obvious. I mean the *integration*. You see, when people say that camels are horses put together by committees, the message is that camels created by committees are bad. They're not. Most of the time those camels are critical to the success of the organization. But a huge amount of critical camel building takes place outside committees as well."

"I don't get it," said Albert.

"My guess is that in most of your life you've acted like a racehorse—focusing on your own strengths, finding the finish line, then racing hell-bent-for-leather toward it without any regard whatsoever for the other horses. That may have worked fine in school. The problem, of course, is that for the projects you're assigned to in the corporate world, it isn't just the completion of one person's work that matters.

Everyone's contribution must come together and all his or her objectives completed in sync for the overall goal to be accomplished.

"Just like the football team," observed Albert.

"Exactly," confirmed the coach. "Group projects and team efforts in organizations have more in common with football games than horse races. The teams that consistently win over time are those where the players help make each other look good. Teams that are carried by a single superstar who looks good at the others' expense never succeed over time. Nor do the individual superstars themselves. The most successful individuals succeed over the long term because they've found a way to leverage their unique talents through others—not because they've outshone them."

By now, the two of them had reached Coach's office. As they sat down, Albert continued the dialogue.

"So that's what you meant when you said camel building can happen outside committees as well as inside them?" asked Albert.

"Exactly," answered the Coach. "Look, let me show you," he said, as he arose from his chair and stood at the chalkboard mounted on the opposite wall.

It was the first time Albert had noticed the old black slate chalkboard hanging on the wall opposite the Coach's desk. *How old is that?* thought Albert. *I wonder where he has to go to find chalk these days. Wow.*

"Let's say you have an objective—a goal you want to accomplish, or a priority. Let's label your objective A," he said as he wrote the letter A on the chalkboard.

A

"Then let's assume your boss has a priority or two. We'll label those priorities BC." He wrote BC in white chalk under the A.

A
B C

The chalk screeched as he wrote the letter C, causing goose bumps to form on Albert's forearms.

"Further, let's assume your boss's boss also has some priorities which I'll call DE." He wrote the letters DE under the BC.

A
B C
D E

"Are you with me?"

"So far," answered Albert.

"Good. Now, for the sake of the metaphor, let's say all

these ideas are good ones—each is a thoroughbred race-horse. You have your horse, your boss has hers, and her boss has his. Whose horse do you bet on?"

"That's not fair," protested Albert.

"Life isn't fair, Albert. Where do you bet?"

"Not on myself, that's for sure. The race is stacked against me."

"No matter how good your idea is, or how important your goals are," explained the Coach.

"So I don't stand a chance," declared Albert.

"Unless you build a camel. Here, look. What happens if you take the time before the race starts and take it upon yourself to build a camel that looks like this?" Coach scrawled the letters BDAEC on the chalkboard.

B A E D C

Albert was relieved that the chalk only screeched once during all five letters. He listened as the Coach continued.

"You then take your camel, BDAEC, to your boss and ask for support in getting the entire proposal accomplished. The first thing she notices is that "B," which is one of her most important priorities is built into your proposal. You tell her that B and C are the framework for the entire proposal, and ask for her support. Do you think she'll give it?"

"Why not? It wouldn't make sense for her not to support a proposal that would lead to the accomplishment of her most important priorities."

"Right. Then you take it to her boss with the same request. What are the odds he'll also support it?"

"Pretty good," said Albert. "For the same reason. He'll be excited that someone is pushing for D and E to be accomplished."

"You got it," exclaimed the Coach as he returned to his seat. "Now. In which case would you prefer to bet on your idea? In the first case where our racehorse, A, is competing by itself with everyone else's, including your boss? Or the second case where your goal is part of the camel you've just created and everyone is pulling for it?"

"The safest bet is the camel," observed Albert.

"By a long shot," confirmed Coach. "And even though your camel may not always be the first to cross the finish line, it will almost always cross. Especially if your boss and hers are both behind it. A lot of racehorses will get lost in the stampede, but a camel almost never will."

"Wow," said Albert.

"But it's not just camel building in committees and with your bosses that matters, Albert. It's also important among your colleagues and co-workers."

"That's why you take time during your practices to let the football players talk and problem solve among themselves," observed Albert.

"That's exactly right. Each player knows what he's trying to accomplish, but doesn't necessarily always think of what the others on the team are trying to achieve. By taking time during each practice to force them to think about working together, we create the habit of camel building. It carries over into our games and almost everything we do."

"Probably even into everything they do after they leave the program and graduate," said Albert.

"Why not? Doesn't it make sense?" asked the Coach.

"Why doesn't everyone do it, then?" countered Albert.

"You tell me," Coach responded.

"I never did it because I didn't know about it. This is the first time I've ever thought about something like this."

"And you really didn't need to think like this until now. It was possible to excel in school by using a different approach."

"I was a racehorse, thinking camels were bad."

"Racehorses aren't bad either, in the right situation. And camel building has its drawbacks. It takes more time. And it also takes more energy. Along with a higher degree of interpersonal skills. But at the end of the day, in most situations, it is more effective," explained the Coach.

"More effective, but not necessarily more efficient," declared Albert.

"Yes, it may take more time, *but frequently the shortcut turns out to be the long cut in the long run, Albert.*"

"I can see that," responded Albert. "And maybe the shortcut turns out to be not effective at all, if you don't accomplish what you've set out to accomplish."

"That's for sure, Albert. Just one more thought. Camel builders are the architects of the future in most companies, because they combine the strengths and vision of everyone on the team to create something everyone can get behind and support. Horses sometimes win and sometimes lose, but in organizations camels always finish in the money." He paused for a moment to let what he said sink in. "Does that give you enough to think about for the day?"

"More than enough. When can we get back together?"

"Two and a half weeks. On Saturday, we have a big game at 1:00. Be here at my office at 10:00 in the morning."

"You got it," Albert responded as he rose to leave. When he reached the door, he paused and turned to the Coach. "And Coach, thanks a lot."

"You're welcome, Albert. I'm glad you're pleased."

Albert was more than pleased. He was absolutely exhilarated. During the drive home his thoughts alternated back and forth between what he was learning and how good it felt to learn it. He tried hard to remember the last time he had experienced this kind of feeling. It was more than just the thrill of having a huge burden lifted from ders, although that was a big part of it. It was also

ore than merely learning something excitingly dif-

ferent, although that was certainly part of it as well. It was like he had just discovered an endless chamber of long-lost buried treasure and he was just beginning to unlock its secrets while savoring the beauty of what lay before him.

Albert felt like he did when he was a kid and had just learned to ride a bike. He remembered how it felt to race up and down and around the dirt paths in the field near his home. He remembered the freedom it gave him to explore places he'd never gone before because they were too far away on foot. He remembered the adventure, the satisfaction, and all the new experiences that came from learning how to ride that bike.

Unbelievably, though, this is better. Not just a little bit better, he surmised, *but orders of magnitude better.* Words were inadequate to describe Albert's joy.

Albert's enthusiasm carried over to his job. The first thing he did upon returning to work, however, was to add several new entries to his electronic journal. He first typed:

Second Secret of Winning Ways:

Camels Are Okay. In fact, today's camel builders will be tomorrow's leaders.

Then he continued typing:

• Some racehorses win and some lose, but a camel will cross the finish line every time.

• Collaboration is better than competition over the long term.

• Camel building should not be left only to committees.

• The shortcut most often turns out to be the long cut in the long run.

As he felt when he reviewed the first secret, Albert thought it would be useful to also bring attention to what the second secret was not about. So he also typed the following:

Camel building does *not* mean:

• Using everyone's suggestion merely to make each person feel good. Camels should be built around goals, objectives, and legitimate needs.

• Everything should be accomplished through a committee.

As the next few days passed, Albert threw himself into his work, trying to build camels at every juncture. Things worked well the first few times he tried it, and he gained more enthusiasm with each effort. Then came Friday.

Albert was assigned a critical project to complete with a short deadline. Because of the complexity of the project, Albert had to team up with a software engineer from another department. *No big deal,* thought Albert. *Time for another camel.*

Albert took the initiative to get the work started, which is something he had never done in the past.

But when he met with Jennifer, the engineer, to outline the project and launch it, trouble started. The problem wasn't that either didn't want to work together, because both did. The problem was that each had a different idea about how the project should be completed. And no matter how hard he tried, Albert just couldn't build a camel. They simply couldn't reach agreement. It wasn't long before each had clearly staked out a definitive position and it became obvious neither would compromise.

Albert was frustrated. He was disillusioned. And he was angry. His first reaction was to blame his frustration on Jennifer. *Why is she being so stubborn? I went to her, acknowledged her abilities, recognized her input, did everything I know how to do to help her feel powerful and strong. Then I tried to build a camel and she got stubborn. Why?*

His next reaction was to blame Coach. *When he gets in*

this kind of situation, he can just tell whoever it is to do what he says. That's how he gets his camels built.

Then he blamed the theory. *It's just like everything else when it comes to people. If everyone does it, it works, but if someone doesn't go along, it's a disaster.*

The longer Albert and Jennifer tried to work out the problem, the worse it got. Albert finally ended the meeting with Jennifer, went back to his office, and banged around on his computer for a while, then left.

Albert's misery persisted throughout the weekend. He randomly went from project to project, but couldn't concentrate on the work at hand. He tried to have fun with Digger, but even that couldn't get his mind off the disaster with Jennifer. Albert just didn't understand what went wrong.

At night Albert tossed and turned, convinced that it was hopeless—he'd never be able to work well with other people. He trudged through the weekend, despondent and dreading having to go back to the office on Monday morning. What was the use? He'd only have to face more conflict, more problems, and the embarrassment of telling Megan that he failed.

On Monday, Albert arrived late to work. Two and a half hours late. He looked distraught. He felt defeated. He was drained. He was sitting at his desk, staring at his computer, when Megan walked into his office.

"Good morning, Albert."

"Hi."

"Everything okay?"

"Who knows."

"Are *you* okay?"

"Who knows."

"Can we talk about it?"

"Whatever."

"I thought we had a meeting scheduled for Friday afternoon to talk about how things are going."

Albert just shrugged his shoulders.

"Did something come up?" asked Megan.

"More like something went down."

"Meaning what?"

"All those great ideas I learned from Coach went down the drain Friday morning."

"Tell me about it," urged Megan.

"There's not much to tell, except that they don't work."

"Excuse me if I push back a bit, Albert, but I happen to know otherwise."

"Well, they sure didn't work Friday."

"Did you tell Coach?"

"I won't see him again until the end of next week, if then."

"What, you think he doesn't have a telephone?"

"Why should I call him? To tell him it doesn't work?"

"He's a coach, Albert. Do you think every play he calls works every time he calls it? He's used to things not working perfectly all the time. And he's used to helping people figure out what went wrong. He's probably wondering why you haven't called him sooner."

Albert thought about this for a minute.

"If I were you, I'd give him a call, Albert. You've got too much at stake." Megan left Albert to think about it some more.

It took Albert about an hour to work up the resolve to telephone Coach. When he finally placed the call, the Coach picked up on the second ring.

"This is Coach."

"Hi, Coach. It's Albert."

"Hey, Albert. How's our rising star doing?"

"I may become your first falling star."

"It can't be that bad. Tell me about it."

And so Albert told him what had happened. The Coach listened to the whole story, only interrupting occasionally to ask clarifying questions. When Albert was completely finished, the Coach responded.

"That's not so bad, Albert."

"Not so bad? It was a total disaster."

"No, a disaster would have been if you had lost your temper or abused someone. At least you didn't treat anyone with a lack of respect. And the real bottom line is that your intentions were noble. All you were trying to do was make things work for both of you. What's so bad about that?"

"What's so bad is that it didn't work," answered Albert.

"A lot of times things don't work on the first attempt, especially when people are involved. But that doesn't make it bad. It just means you have to figure out how to make it work. The important thing is that your intentions are noble. I'm sure Jennifer's are, too."

"So how do I make it work?"

"The key is something we haven't had a chance to talk about yet."

"I'm all ears," said Albert.

"Good," answered Coach. "I'll tell you what. What time do you have?"

"About 3:30."

"Good. Do you know where Inspiration Point is?"

"About halfway between here and UNM, but over by the shore, near that hilly area."

"That's it. I'll meet you there at 5:30."

"Today?" asked Albert.

"In two hours," said the Coach.

"Okay."

"See you there."

It was a beautiful afternoon and Albert enjoyed the hour-and-a-half drive to Inspiration Point. The leaves were just beginning to turn and the whole area was beautiful.

He arrived a few minutes before 5:30 and walked over

to the lookout point while he waited for the Coach. The view was absolutely magnificent. He stood high on a bluff looking out at the water stretching expansively to the west. Albert watched the graceful flight of a beautiful, white gull as it soared along, riding the strong but gentle updrafts along the face of the bluff. *This really is phenomenal,* thought Albert. *No wonder they call it Inspiration Point.*

Just as Albert's gaze shifted to track the flight of another gull gliding along the updrafts, the muffled roar of an automobile engine drew his attention back to where he had parked his Saturn. He looked back just in time to see a silver convertible with its top down fly into the parking area like a NASCAR racing car pulling into a pit stop. Albert glanced at his wrist watch. Five-thirty on the dot. Coach was at the wheel. He was wearing leather driving gloves, stylish dark glasses, a racing jacket with matching beret, and a long scarf that hung back from around his neck and into the back seat. Albert did a double take to make sure it was Coach. It was indeed.

The coach nimbly exited his car and walked toward Albert. "I see you made it, Albert."

"Uh, yeah."

"What do you think?"

"About this place? It's really neat."

"It's beautiful, isn't it?"

"I was just thinking how phenomenal it really is," observed Albert.

"Tell me, Albert. You've obviously been enjoying the scenery for a while. Which is more beautiful, the water or the land?"

Albert thought for a moment. "That's a tough one, Coach."

"The sky or the shore?"

"I don't really know. I guess each has its own beauty."

"There's a point here, Albert. It's about how we think about certain things."

Albert turned all his attention to the coach.

"Semanticists—those are the people who study the impact of words and language on people—have made an interesting observation about those of us who have been born and raised in Western cultures," explained the Coach.

"What's that?" asked Albert.

"In Western society we are taught to think about almost everything as being either right or wrong. We almost never think of things as being part right or part wrong or a mix of both."

"Um-huh," said Albert, thinking deeply about the implications of Coach's message.

"Or we might think of things as good or bad. Again, it's either one or the other. Like night or day. It can never be both. In essence, we use either/or thinking rather than a more appropriate multi-valued orientation," explained the Coach.

"What do you mean by multi-valued?" asked Albert.

"Very few decisions you'll face in the corporate world are two-valued decisions—by that I mean choices between right and wrong or good and bad. When you do face those kinds of decisions, your choices will be reasonably straight-forward. You'll decide and move on without much deliberation or struggle. What you'll learn is that most of the difficult choices you'll face in the workplace will be multi-valued choices."

"I don't know what that means," said Albert.

"Consider an example. Let's say you are deciding which piece of lab equipment to buy to satisfy a specific need you have on a project. Just to keep it simple, let's assume you have two choices."

"Okay," said Albert, following the example.

"The first choice can be purchased from Vendor #1 for $500. The equipment can be delivered in a month, but will be supported by local technicians supplied by the company. And it has a two-year warranty. The second choice can be purchased from Vendor #2 for $700. It can be delivered in forty-eight hours, but the company doesn't provide local technical support. If problems arise, the equipment will need to be shipped back to the plant where they guarantee a seventy-two-hour turnaround. It has a three-year warranty. Which vendor do you buy from, #1 or #2?"

"I don't know," answered Albert.

"Nor do I," said the Coach. "The point is that there is no one best answer that is completely right or completely wrong. The best answer depends upon the circumstances. For example, if I have my own in-house technicians, then local support is less important to me. Likewise the longer warranty. But if I have an urgent need, the forty-eight-hour delivery might be critical, compared to waiting a month."

"So it all depends on the situation," observed Albert.

"And most situations you'll encounter on the job will have a number of factors that enter into the equation—just like the situation we're encountering here." The sun was starting to set over the water, making the already magnificent view even more spectacular.

"I get it," said Albert. "You asked me two-valued questions like which is nicer, *either* the water *or* the land, and it really wasn't appropriate."

"Right," replied the Coach. "All the elements contribute to the overall beauty in their own special way. They're neither good nor bad, nor is one better than the other. The same logic applies to the situation you now face with Jennifer."

"How do you mean?" asked Albert.

"You approached the project from your point of view, thinking it was the right way, and she approached it from hers, just as convinced that hers was the best way. It was a little bit like what would happen if you and I sat here and argued over which was more beautiful—the sky or the shore. You were arguing about the wrong thing. Both of you got hung up on who was right and who was wrong, or whose approach was good and whose was bad, and you lost sight of the fact that it wasn't either/or."

"What should I have done then?"

"The next time it happens, you can call time out. Rather than continue to butt heads over one way or the other, go back to the beginning. Reach agreement on all the different criteria you need to satisfy, then work toward a solution that satisfies those criteria."

"Satisfies the criteria rather than one or the other of *us*," offered Albert.

"It's not about egos. It should never be about *who* is right and *who* is wrong. It shouldn't even be about *what* is right or wrong. It's about doing what's best given the complexities you face."

"So two-valued thinking is a trap," observed Albert.

"But it's a trap we've been conditioned to fall into our entire lives because it's all around us. Our legal system is based on a two-valued premise—people are either guilty or not guilty. Its the same with most religions—our actions are either a sin or not a sin. Even in school, teachers look for answers that are either right or wrong. Most students' answers are considered to be either completely right or completely wrong, with not much in between. Then, to make matters worse as we get older, we translate everything into ego. It's no longer *the answer* that's right or wrong; it's *me.*"

"I guess I do that a lot."

"We all do it more than we should," explained the Coach.

"So how do we change it?" asked Albert.

"Our only hope is to change ourselves first," answered the Coach. "We can start by changing the way we think. Now that you know about the two-valued thinking trap, you'll be amazed at how often it appears—not only in your own thinking, but everywhere around you. Once you recognize it, it'll be fairly easy to avoid falling into it. But a good place for you to start might be with Jennifer. What do you think?"

"It just might work. I want to think about it some more tonight and try it out tomorrow," said Albert just as the sun melted into the horizon.

"Sounds like a great plan. Let me know if you have any questions."

"I will, Coach. And thanks again."

Albert watched as the coach donned his leather racing gloves along with the rest of his driving paraphernalia, slid in behind the wheel of the shiny silver convertible and raced off into the twilight.

Albert's mind spun during the drive back as he digested yet another principle. He was back to being excited again about what he was learning. As soon as he arrived back at the office he immediately accessed his learning journal and began typing.

Third Secret of Winning Ways:

Avoid Two-Valued Thinking
Traps, because very few decisions are
choices between right and wrong or
good and bad.

Then, as before, he typed still more:

• *Keep egos out of it.* It's not *who's* right or
wrong. It's usually not even *what's* right or
wrong. More often than not it's what is *best*
under the circumstances.

• *Most decisions are multi-valued, depending
upon the situation.*

• *Almost every situation can be analyzed prop-
erly if viewed from a variety of perspectives.*

Once again, Albert wanted to outline the flip side of the
issue to make sure he fully captured his newfound knowledge. So he also typed:

In avoiding two-valued thinking traps,
be careful of the following:

• Avoid Analysis Paralysis. Don't bring so many variables into play that you can't reach a conclusion.

• Avoid Indecisiveness. Looking at multiple variables isn't an excuse to avoid being decisive.

• Remember that some decisions are two-valued. When choosing whether or not to act according to your personal ethics or the values of the organization, more often than not these are decisions between right and wrong.

Albert reflected for a while on what he had written, then went home. He stopped and bought Digger some of his favorite treats on the way. They took a long, fun walk as Albert planned how to apply this new knowledge. Thoughts about how he would approach Jennifer the next day danced around in his head until he finally dozed off around midnight.

The next morning he tracked Jennifer down first thing. He apologized for what had happened the previous Friday and asked if they could spend some time looking at the project through fresh eyes. Although it was clear she wasn't teeming with enthusiasm, she at least agreed.

Their meeting got off to a bumpy start, but after they got into it, Albert's enthusiasm for looking at the project in a different way—one they could both embrace—became contagious. They accomplished more than he had predicted, and both felt good when they finished.

Toward the end of the meeting, Albert happened to mention Digger. Albert had never shared anything about his personal life with anyone at work before. Jennifer was intrigued. They laughed out loud together when Albert told her about the time Digger had chased a Frisbee right into the middle of a young family's freshly laid out picnic lunch at the beach. Albert was animated and enjoyed making Jennifer giggle. *She must actually think I'm funny!* Albert thought. His heart nearly skipped a beat when she told Albert she looked forward to their next meeting.

No one has ever said that to me before, thought Albert. He found himself looking forward to their next meeting as well.

The pace of Albert's work picked up considerably. Albert was having more fun and he was accomplishing more. He and Jennifer had a few more meetings that went well. And soon their working relationship blossomed into a warm friendship. The time literally flew by until it was time for Albert to visit Coach again at Saturday's game.

Albert woke up before dawn on Saturday morning.

He popped out of bed and into the shower full of anticipation. He shaved, brushed his teeth, dressed in a heavy sweater with matching corduroy trousers and a scarf with the school colors, and was out the door in fifteen minutes.

He was excited, but also nervous. Until now all his meetings had been with only the Coach. Today he expected to be closer to the team and the other staff members. *I wonder how they'll accept me,* thought Albert. *They're probably leery of outsiders—especially someone who hasn't had much to do with football. What if I do something dumb in front of them?*

The drive took the usual three hours, even with Albert stopping at a fast food place along the way for a breakfast sandwich and some orange juice.

At 10:30 he walked into Coach's office.

"Good morning, Albert."

"Hi, Coach."

"Glad to see you're wearing our colors,"

Albert was surprised that the coach was wearing almost the same thing as Albert, except he didn't have a scarf. And his shoes were different. At practice, Coach wore a pair of black cleats. But the shoes he was wearing today were something else.

They were old tennis shoes. Albert guessed they must have been at least thirty years old, maybe older. They were black and white, although the black had faded to almost gray, and they were ankle high. New white shoestrings were laced criss-cross from the toes to the ankles. Closer scrutiny revealed that the shoes must have been patched a number of times during their lifetime. It even appeared as though some of the round, metal eyelets for the shoelaces had been replaced. Most of the knobs around the edges of the rubber soles were worn smooth and when Coach rested his left foot on the outer edge of the sole, it appeared most of the tread had long since been worn smooth. Coach noticed Albert staring at the shoes.

"The shoes are kind of a 'thing' around here," commented the Coach.

"Looks like they have been for quite some time," observed Albert.

"Ever since the very first game I coached," explained Coach. "I was anxious and uptight, scurrying around trying to get everything ready, and I misplaced my only coaching shoes. I only had one pair of street shoes then that I used for teaching and going places. And these. They were old even then. But it was raining and muddy so I decided it would be better to wear these than my other good shoes. So I did. The game was a mess. We didn't do much right at all. But in the fourth quarter, several huge breaks came our way and we won the game. Afterward in the locker room, everyone was covered with mud and tired, but incredibly happy. Back then the school hadn't won a game in almost two years. Because we couldn't have won without the breaks there at the end, everyone said it was the shoes. They said it was Coach's good-luck shoes that changed football forever at UNM."

"And they still say that?"

"Some of the old-time storytellers. Mostly what people close to the team say is that our winning ways are what wins games, but they still want the shoes just in case. It gives us something special to identify with. It also ties our past to the present and helps create a common vision."

"A common vision?"

"It sounds a little esoteric, but it's the term I like to use. And it's the basis for our final secret."

"Wait a minute," Albert requested as he pulled a pen and a small note pad with a wire spiral binding across the top from his back pocket. "If we're going to start talking about the last secret, I want to take notes."

"Good," responded the Coach. "Because there are a number of different things to think about with secret number four."

"I'm all ears," said Albert.

"Let's start with common vision."

"Sounds good," responded Albert, writing the words on his note pad.

"Simply stated, this means to know where you're headed, know where the organization is headed, and know where everyone around you is headed. Then you work with them to create a common direction or purpose. You make sure that the vision everyone focuses on for the future is a shared or common vision."

"If you're working on a project with someone, shouldn't it be obvious you're both trying to achieve the same thing?" asked Albert.

"That assumption can get you into trouble," explained the Coach.

"Why?" asked Albert.

"Very rarely do individuals or groups approach a task with the exact same goal in mind. Usually everyone has a slightly different view of the way things should turn out. This isn't good or bad, it just is. It's usually the way things work because everyone wants something different out of life and career, and even the job at hand."

"Doesn't everyone want to do a good job and be successful?" asked Albert.

"Usually, but success can be defined in many ways. For some people, success means gaining recognition. Others may be looking for happiness or fulfillment. Still others may have a burning desire to excel. Take our football team, for example."

"Everyone wants to win," said Albert.

"It's not quite that simple."

"Why not?"

"Of course everyone wants the team to win, but sometimes certain individuals might have personal goals that are so important to them that they might give those goals a higher priority than winning. A player who hasn't played much this year just might want to get into the game for a few plays. Another player who made a mistake last week might want to redeem himself this week. Still another might be looking to set a personal record or achieve a statistical milestone."

"And if everyone pursued their personal goals at the expense of the team, the team would suffer. You'd lose sight of the overall goal at the expense of each team member's self-interest," observed Albert.

"It's possible," agreed the Coach. "A great professional football coach I once knew had an interesting philosophy that we've adopted here. He said that after each game his teams won or lost, he either celebrated the victory or mourned the loss for twenty-four hours. Then he cleared those emotions from his mind and got everyone to focus on the next game."

"Wow."

"That's the fourth secret: Influence for the Future, rather than the present or the past."

"You're going to have to explain it in more detail," said Albert.

"There are basically three elements to influencing for the future that are critical," explained the Coach. "The first we've already talked about to some extent, and it's the basis for the other two. It is to develop a common vision. Make sure you and anyone you're working with are working toward goals and purposes that are in alignment. The worst thing that can happen is to start working with someone only to find out later you were at cross purposes."

"I can relate to that," agreed Albert. "In fact I've done that a lot and it's been frustrating."

"The second element is to solve problems in the future."

"What do you mean?" asked Albert, as he continued to take copious notes.

"When a lot of people try to solve problems they look backward rather than forward. They get into a lot of 'he said/she said' discussions that only create hard feelings and more confusion. It's much better to look ahead. Ask questions like 'how can we prevent problems like this from occurring in the future?' and 'how can we remove any obstacles that stand in the way of achieving our goal?' "

"If you look to the future, then you're also not blaming anyone for what happened in the past," interjected Albert.

"Great insight, Albert. Blame is the biggest obstacle to effective problem solving there is. Because you see, at the end of the day, it doesn't matter who did what to whom when. The only thing that matters is whether or not we'll be able to accomplish our goals for tomorrow."

"I can see that," said Albert.

"During our team practices each week we don't dwell on the mistakes that were made the previous week. We focus on what it will take to win next week. Sure, if someone made a mistake the previous week, we'll help them learn from it, but always in the context of what it will take to win the next game. If the mistake a player made last week won't matter next week, we don't even talk about it."

"Got it," said Albert, continuing to write.

"The same with plays that don't work. We don't try to make someone feel guilty or blame anybody if a play didn't work last week. What we want to know is whether or not it will work next week. Next week will be a different opponent—that means completely different players, strengths, and weaknesses. It doesn't do any good to replay last week's game against next week's opponent."

"Just like it wouldn't make sense to approach our next Tiger Team project the same way we approached the last one."

"Exactly."

"All this makes sense, Coach. But we started this whole conversation by talking about your old tennis shoes, and I'm still not clear how they tie into all this."

"Ah. Of course," answered the Coach with a hearty chuckle. "You don't miss a thing, Albert."

Albert smiled as he waited for the Coach to continue.

"The shoes help us to create a special sense of identity and allegiance that goes beyond just being members of the same team. They have become a symbol of our tradition— a tradition that, quite honestly, is bigger than all of us. But it's a tradition that gives every member of our team a special shared identity. It's a special identity we share with every player who has ever worn our colors for the past twenty-two years."

The coach was somber as he continued. "Some people think it's the luck that's stored in the shoes that helps us win in difficult situations. It's not luck. Before each game I talk to the team about our tradition and how those shoes have carried us through some tough times. I remind the players that those shoes represent a bond that exists between us and all the other teams who have gone before. I explain how blessed we are to be part of something so special and how important it is, that no matter how bad things might be going, it's up to us to rise above the challenges of the moment and bring honor to those who have gone before us and to each and every one who is a member of this special group, carrying forward this special tradition. All teams have uniforms, colors, and mascots, but no other team anywhere has the same quality of shared identity that we have. These shoes are our game day reminder of that specialness."

"Wow," commented Albert. "Will I be able to hear you address the team?"

"Sorry, Albert."

Albert immediately understood. He was sorry he let his exuberance put the Coach on the spot that way. It wouldn't honor the tradition to have him intrude.

ut," Coach continued, "you'll certainly be able to
share in the results. You are staying for the game,
aren't you?"

"I don't think I'll miss another UNM game as long as
I live, as long as you're the coach," beamed Albert.

The team won that day 35 to 11.

Digger was delighted when Albert re-
turned home that evening. The two went for a long walk
until almost midnight. Then Albert logged on his network
from his home computer and added the following to his
winning ways learning journal.

Fourth Secret of Winning Ways:

Influence for the Future, rather
than the present or the past.

Then he added:

• *Develop a common vision with your colleagues.*
Ensure all your efforts are aligned with a
common sense of purpose and clear goals
for your efforts.

- *Solve problems in the future.* Don't blame and criticize others for things that happened in the past. Remove obstacles that stand in the way of future achievement.

- *Create a shared sense of identity and responsibility.* Going one step beyond alignment, it is important that people also invest in the success of your joint efforts.

And, as he had done before, Albert felt it important to capture what the fourth secret was not. So he added:

Influencing in the future does *not* mean:

- Ignoring present realities. Everything you focus on for the future should be grounded in reality and take into account your current capabilities as well as limitations.

- Ignoring the lessons of the past. Experience can be the best teacher of all if we learn the right lessons from our experience. The key is to learn what we can and then apply what we've learned to our future success.

The next morning when he woke up, Digger was waiting next to Albert's bed with his favorite Frisbee in his mouth. The two went for a romp in the park, then Albert went to church.

On his way home Albert's mind was still racing with all he had learned. He was happy and excited, and wanted nothing more than to share his exuberance with someone.

On an impulse, he pulled into the parking lot of a convenience store. He parked his car near the phone booth that was located on one end of the building. It only took a minute to get the information operator on the line and get the phone number he wanted to call. He dropped a few coins in the slot and dialed. After three rings a pleasant female voice came on the line.

"Hello."

"Jennifer?"

"Yes?"

"It's me, uh, Albert."

"Oh. Hi, Albert. Is something up with our project?"

"No, nothing like that. I was just thinking. I'm going to take Digger for a walk on the beach, and thought you might like to go."

"You mean, like right now?"

"Well, if it's convenient. But yeah, I was thinking pretty soon, so maybe we could spend most of the afternoon together. I mean if you don't have something better to do or anything like that."

"I'd love to."

"You would?"

"I've been dying to meet Digger."

"You have?"

"I've told you how much I love dogs."

All of a sudden Albert couldn't think of what to say next. He was panicked.

"Are you still there?" she asked.

"Uh, yeah."

"Do you want me to meet you and Digger somewhere? Or do you want to come by my apartment? I'm pretty sure it's on the way."

"Uh, yeah. I remember where you told me it is. We'll pick you up in about an hour."

"See you soon."

"Bye."

When Albert hung up, his heart was pounding at a rate that was at least three times faster than normal. He could hardly breathe. He hadn't expected to feel this way. He was only looking for someone to talk to and share his excitement with. Now he was so excited, he couldn't stand it.

He got back into his car, grabbed the steering wheel with both hands, and just stared forward for three long minutes. He finally managed to get his feelings back under control, but just barely.

He drove home carefully, even though he felt like he was floating on clouds. When he came through the front door, Digger immediately noticed the bounce in Albert's step and the energy that radiated from him in all directions. Albert was actually singing out loud! Digger joined right in, barking and yipping, jumping and skipping, sharing the full extent of Albert's newfound joy.

The autumn weather made it too cold for sunning or playing in the surf, but that didn't rule out a picnic. So Albert loaded his ice chest along with a few blankets and the Frisbee into the trunk of his Saturn. And they were off.

He stopped at the local supermarket. While Digger waited anxiously in the car, Albert purchased an expensive bottle of Cabernet Sauvignon, a bottle of Chardonnay, some cheese, a couple of baguettes, three pears, a couple of large delicious apples, and a five-pound bag of party ice. At the last minute he threw in a bag of potato chips just in case. He also bought a nice bouquet of flowers arranged in a reed basket to use as a centerpiece. He smiled as realized he'd never done anything like this before.

In just a few short minutes he had the Chardonnay buried in ice in the cooler with the fruit and cheese resting coolly on top. He closed the trunk and in a flash, he and Digger were off to Jennifer's.

Jennifer was waiting out front when they arrived. As soon as he saw her, Albert's heart started pounding.

Albert parked at the curb in front of her and quickly

let Digger out so they could get acquainted. They connected instantly.

After playing around briefly, they all loaded into the Saturn and headed for the shore. Their excitement was genuine as Albert told Jennifer what he had learned and how much he wanted to share it with her. Digger only added to the fun as he kept poking his head up between the front seats to gain attention and seek affection.

When they arrived at Albert's favorite beach, Albert showed Jennifer the picnic fixings he had thrown together. She couldn't have been more excited if he had taken her to the most expensive Cordon Bleu restaurant in Chicago.

They picnicked and played Frisbee. They talked about the winning ways, but they also talked about each other. They laughed and they shared. And they bonded.

During the next few months Jennifer and Albert completed their project to rave reviews.

The following spring each was made project manager of a different Tiger Team. The two teams successfully tackled two of the most important projects at UGAT.

Then in June, Jennifer and Albert were married. Digger was the ring bearer, using a special satin pillow strapped to his back.

Together they continued to develop winning ways,

finding the techniques to be valuable in both their personal and professional lives. They found that by sharing these ideas with friends and colleagues, they were able to help others develop winning relationships every bit as powerful as their own.

the end

DICK LYLES

Dick Lyles is President and Chief Operating Officer of The Ken Blanchard Companies, a full-service consulting and performance improvement company headquartered in Escondido, CA. He has had a distinguished career as an entrepreneur, executive, author, speaker, and consultant with international clientele for more than twenty-five years. His clients have included companies of all sizes, including many Fortune 500 companies and government agencies at all levels around the world.

He has authored or co-authored several books, the most recent of which is *Responsible Managers Get Results* (AMACOM), co-authored with Gerry Faust and Will Phillips. His training program, *Problems and Decisions,* has been offered in seventeen different countries, on six continents, and in nine languages.

Dick is a frequent guest on radio and television programs and speaks at conventions, conferences, and executive retreats around the world.

With his wife, Martha, he founded Maric College in San Diego, CA, where he served as president for three and a half years and Chairman of the Board for another eight. Maric is an accredited paramedical school for training nurses and allied health professionals.

Whether he is delivering a keynote address, consulting with clients, coaching protégés, or leading his management team, Dick Lyles is known for his ability to energize people and develop powerful, results-producing relationships—in essence, he "walks the talk" of *Winning Ways.*